b. r. fleming

traces . . .

After Thought Publications

First published 2023.

ISBN: 978-0-9838201-3-0

Imagery: BRImagery
Cover/Book Design: J R Fleming

ATTENTION: SCHOOLS AND BUSINESSES
AfterThought Publications materials are available
at quantity discounts with bulk purchase for educational,
business, or sales promotional use. For information,
please email the author @ brflemingauthor@gmail.com.

a poetry collection . . .

1

summer's breeze enfolds,
breathes life, awakens!
harbors, energizes the soul . . .

sea meets sky meets earth,
mind meets soul meets self,
the encompassing universe . . .

there you are
here i am
miles and hours
in between . . .

autumn brings comfort
cool breezes lift the spirits
invigorating . . .

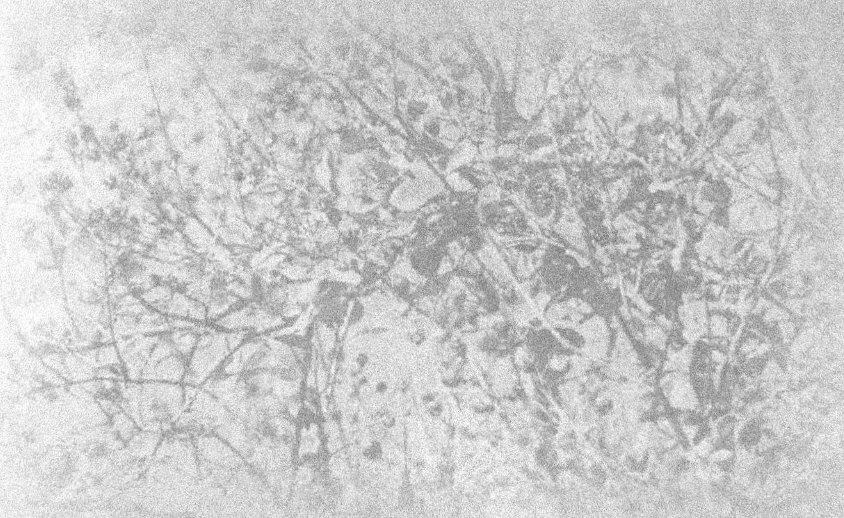

the rain softly falls,
glistening on the faint leaves,
renewing the earth . . .

the sky opens up,
reveals its splendid expanse,
my heart leaps for joy . . .

September and hot
a cooler climate beckons
oceans, rivers, springs . . .

clouds block the hot sun
a momentary respite
the sun will win though . . .

pale clouds fill the sky
a cool breeze chills the eggplant
autumn approaches . . .

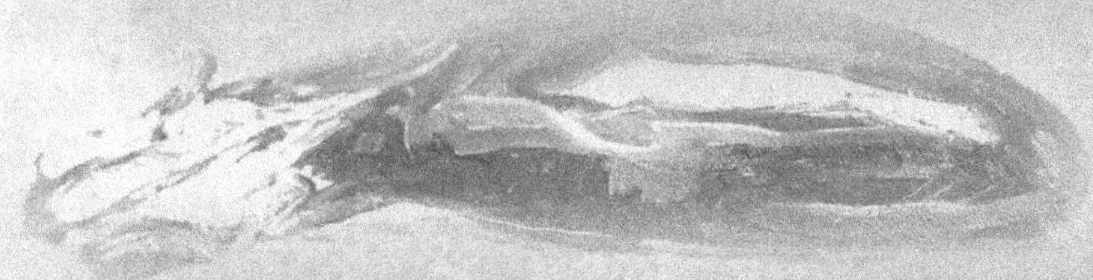

nectar fills the aloe leaves
water only when needed
a diaphanous ambrosia . . .

some live and some die
the lifeforce ebbs and flows
indiscriminate . . .

glistening water
warm sunshine energizes
winter disappears . . .

ducks sallying forth
surfing the rippling waves
nature having fun . . .

mountains outline sky
sky claims blue, one wispy cloud
natural world . . .

vastness of the sky
tweaks the imagination
other worldly . . .

does love live within?
nestled in darkest corners
flirting with the moon . . .

the end has drawn nigh
summer promises rebirth
a new beginning . . .

waves of blue and white
bending to another will
if only they could see . . .

flitting tree to tree
endless fruitful scavenging
a murder of crows . . .

though we are apart,
you invade my every thought,
my soul yearns for you . . .

the rain softly falls,
glistening on the faint leaves,
renewing the earth . . .

the sultry sea moans,
a captivating ardor,
mesmerizing you . . .

to write is to live,
to not write is death,
life and death
balancing on words . . .

look! the flame ignites!
sizzles! glows! ablaze!
soon, ultimately,
extinguished . . .

the tense sea beckons,
captures your being,
brands, mends,
simultaneously . . .

Mother Nature thrives
birds fly, lizards scurry,
ducks surf waves
life striving at the lake . . .

waves crash on the shore,
move earth and sand to and fro,
ending a moment . . .

28

the heat bakes my skin
the fan disturbs the warm air
night may bring coolness . . .

the plants need water
the heat has drained their juices
the eggplant wilted . . .

the fireplace light shines
evening begins again
night promises rest . . .

what time of day now
dusk or dawn,
does it matter?
they blend together . . .

32

clouds shade the red sun
the eerie haze fills the day
the sweet mint blossoms . . .

bees attack blossoms
fulfill their solemn duty
nectar for the hive . . .

brown leaves and green leaves
life and death coexisting
on a single branch . . .

bees seeking nectar
yellow butterflies flitter
fuchsia flowers call . . .

time slips slowly by
leaving only memories
living thoughts of you . . .

blackbirds sing their song
fill the afternoon stillness
awaiting nightfall . . .

seeing you here, now
catapults my emotions
delivers the cure . . .

Miles' trumpet beckons
calls forth buried emotions
enriches my soul . . .

the trumpet charms me
entreats me to play along
frolicking with my mind . . .

fan! Fan! cool me down!
raising the hairs on my legs
promising relief . . .

my car just sits there
awaiting my next presence
the dust likes the view . . .

beside the aloe plant
mister potatohead waves
a staid reminder . . .

sunshine warms the day
glistening waves reflect rays
the coming of spring . . .

the fan rests, silent
awaits the afternoon sun
clouds have no intent . . .

thinking still of you
though desperate miles divide
do you think of me? . . .

ice, plenty of ice
cooling the insides with ice
the outside still burns . . .

eggplants have sprouted
cherry tomatoes cluster
peppers venture forth . . .

49

Miles' tones stir my soul
the brewing bitches enthrall
and lull the demon . . .

caring and gentle,
enfolded in loving arms,
the babe smiles gleefully . . .

my love is so fair,
my heart sings to think of her,
a love with no end . . .

cloudy today
a little chilly
you say its warm
maybe it is
where you are
can you feel the goosebumps?

love pulverized me!
pummeled me, breathless
and escaped!
emptiness remains . . .

54

tree trimming today
the crows trumpet their complaints
nature wins in time . . .

greens, yellows, browns, reds
nature painting a scene
my purple toe blends in . . .

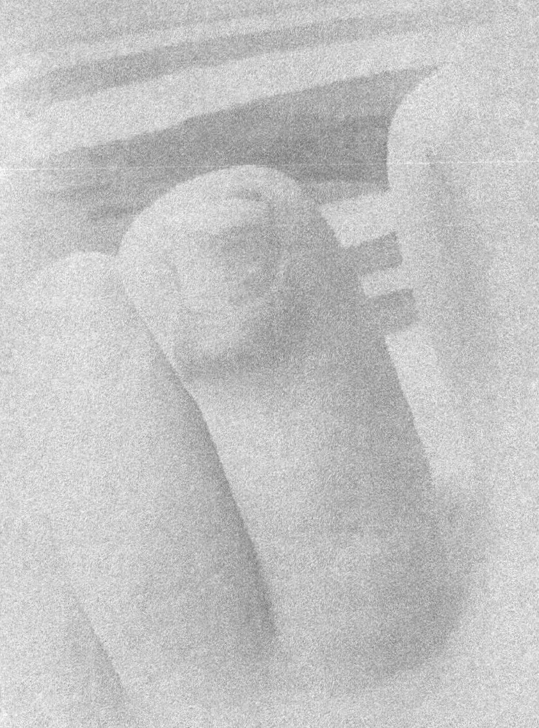

bees buzzing the blooms
butterflies flittering by
the hummingbird waits . . .

new seedlings sprouting
surging forth toward the sun
do the others slumber? . . .

the wind swirls through
playing the wind chime's eerie tune
nature's symphony . . .

the new juice sparkles
a hummingbird sips the liquor
a dinner for one . . .

The Cure fill the bowl
Robert Smith imparts his spell
boundless joy erupts . . .

the music loft rests, silent
bass guitars feel neglected
forgotten tones remain . . .

a black crow takes flight
another follows the flight plan
a wreckless journey . . .

my love is a rose,
with thorns that prick with soft sighs,
a sweet and sour blend . . .

waiting fills my days
longing to see you again
hope has no future . . .

time persists, endless
knowing all, revealing none
tormenting lovers . . .

Also by B. R. Fleming

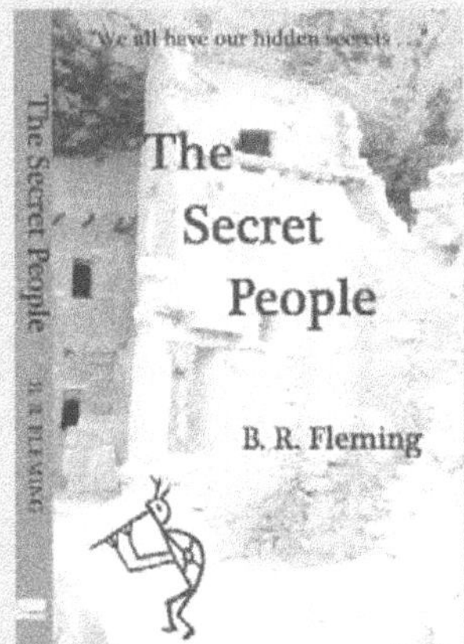

Available from Amazon and other book retailers.

Follow B. R. Fleming:

Amazon: https://tinyurl.com/224h2fbn
Twitter: @BFScreenwriter
Instagram: brfleming_write_play_shoot
Facebook: www.facebook.com/bruce.fleming49
Website: http://brflemingauthor.wix.com/brfleming
Email: brflemingauthor@gmail.com

www.ingramcontent.com/pod-product-compliance
Lightning Source LLC
LaVergne TN
LVHW021201160826
845679LV00024B/2202